OUR JOURNEY ON EARTH

CHANDRA KARNA

Durgadas Karna

Our journey on Earth is like a train of life, with its stations, changes of routes, and accidents. At birth we met our parents and boarded the train and believed they will always travel with us. However, at some station our parents will step down the train, leaving us on this journey alone.

As time goes by, other people will board the train and they will be significant i.e., our siblings, friends, and even the love of our life. Many will step down and leave a vacuum, others will go so unnoticed that we do not realise that they vacated their seats, which is very sad when you think of it. Have a good relationship with your co-passengers. We do not know when we will stepdown leaving the seat vacant.

Today is the day when my beloved husband left us, it is 8th of May 2021, at 11 o'clock at night, so I thought I will put down few words for him, so that my children, grandchildren and friends will remember him.

My life with him was a challenging one, as if God was judging me to the extent I could bear the difficulties we faced together.

Who are we, from where have we all come, nobody knows, but this much is certain that there is a super power who is controlling us. Many a times you must have observed that when we are about to do something wrong, there is always a warning, a thought in your mind, some sort of warning telling you not to do it. This is God who is guiding you, but at times we are stubborn and do not listen to the warning and land into trouble. God has sent us to perform our duty, which each one of us should do honestly.

I always had that feeling right from childhood that I am sent to perform my duty well. Duty first towards parents who have brought me up, then in laws and the rest of the people around me.

The clock is ticking away, it is doing its duty by going on and on. We should take advantage and do our duty well too, who knows I might not be there to finish what I came on this Earth for. So, make the most of each moment.

God sent me to perform my duty towards my loving husband, my in laws, who had multiple health problems in their lives. This habit I picked up from my father, who went to the hospital after office hours, to look after the injured during World War II. This same feeling of helping people in distress, came to me.

Chatu and myself with my parents and Dinesh and Satya

I used to see my mom work — the kitchen, cooking delicious food for all of us. So right from the age of 13 I used to help her in cooking. From then onwards cooking was my passion. My husband loved my cooking and I took pains to prepare new recipes for him. He was always the first one to taste whatever new dish I made.

My sweet husband was born in Sindh in 1934 to his two wonderful parents Shri Menghraj Karna and Smt Putli Karna. They must have been overjoyed as he was born after 3 daughters. Then came another daughter after him. I can imagine how overjoyed his sisters would have been when they took their small tiny brother in their arms for the first time. His four sisters Mohini didi, Padma didi, Papu didi and Usha showered all their love on him. He was a pampered child. Then came along myself when he was 30 years old and I too pampered him.

Chatu with his parents

He was such a nice person, very good at heart. He would say we all are born with good qualities; nobody is born bad. He was patient and soft spoken. I never heard him shout or hit our children and both of my children are like him. We walked hand in hand and overcame the hurdles of life together.

He would always say, when you can resolve differences amicably why fight and argue, and destroy your relationship. Just show your back to the person who hurts you and ignore that person. But I am not like him. I would harp on it or analyse as to why that person was rude to me. He would say that is his or her karma.

He had a heart of gold. He would say let the palm of your hand be down and not up, meaning if your palm is down then you are at the giving end and if it is up meaning you are asking for something. We both were happy with what little we had.

The two of us

As far as honesty goes, he was too honest in his work in C.P.W.D. He worked on construction sites for 22 years. He worked so hard to finish the projects given to him in time. One of his projects in Delhi was water treatment plant in Shahdara. In a way the first assignment that he got in 1965 was the construction of Sonali Pokhran road in Nepal. It took the Indian workers 5 years to finish the road of 140 km stretch. We lived in jungles as we proceeded to build the road in the interiors.

The beginning of the Sonali-Pokran road was from Nautanwa near Gorakhpur. Nepal is a hilly country so we had to cut mountain sides. We built temporary houses wherever we went into the interior, with 3 to 4 families living together. We stayed at every station for a year and then proceeded further into the interior, slowly cutting our way. Life was hard, as we got only Dal, Rice, Atta and Sugar from Gorakhpur. The last station was near the Nepal border. Regarding vegetables we got them from the local people. Pure ghee was in abundance. We shared whatever we had and lived a comfortable life. We stayed in 5 different places in Nepal, last being Pokhran.

We came back to India in May 1970. Satya our 2nd son was born on 28th June, 1970. My father-in-law was so happy. He said he prayed for another grandson. My husband was the only son in their families. His 2 masi's did not have sons.

Both my children are the mirror image of their father, soft spoken, honest, very generous, speak very less too. They have inherited all these qualities from their grandfather and father. My father-in-law was a gem of a person. A man of few words. He was a lawyer. His eyes would tell you what he needed. If asked he would say yes or no by nodding.

After coming back from Nepal, my husband was soon posted to Bangalore with a promotion. We were given a bungalow in Upper Palace Orchard, being the only executive engineer in Bangalore. He worked till late sometimes as we lived on the first floor and the office was on the ground floor. We were there for 5 years. Dinesh, the older one was to go to 6th standard when we were posted back to Delhi in 1976.

Every year I would bring my children to Delhi in summer vacation to see their grandparents. They used to be so happy to see them. After returning from Bangalore and being posted to Delhi we stayed together in joint family for many years.

The four of us at Lajpat Nagar

As time went by children grew up. Dinesh went to engineering college at BITS Pilani and Satya to Pondicherry for MBBS. When Satya was in 10th class, Chatu, as my hubby was called was posted in Yemen. There they had to build houses for Yemenese who had lost their homes in the earthquake.

Sanaa is the capital of South Yemen. His main office was in Sanaa, but he had to go to the site everyday to supervise the work. After 8-10 months he called Dinesh to Yemen. Then after some time Satya & I went there. There I found that hard work that he was doing looking after multiple sites, was not good for his health. I asked him to come back to India but he would not listen, saying he wanted to finish the work. But God had other plans for him. He had a massive heart attack in office one day with the result he was in ICU for 3 weeks, and 3 weeks rest at home, then he was allowed to come back to India.

In the ICU at Sanaa, one of the nurses from Kerala had worked under my sister-in-law, Mohini Karna in Holy Family Hospital, Delhi. She was such a sweet person and she looked after him so well throughout his stay in the ICU. Unfortunately, there were no medical facilities in Yemen, not even an ECG.

We returned after 6 weeks to Bombay and went for check up at Jaslok Hospital. Angiography was done. The results showed one artery completely blocked and he was suggested bypass surgery.

We were then suggested to go to the USA for the surgery in the month of March 1988. We left for Chicago where Dr. Ramesh Chabblani and nine other doctors looked at his history. They all said that there was no need for the surgery but to take half a tablet of aspirin daily. His diet should be light and simple with less oil & salt, no masalas and no red chillies.

Can you believe that he lived a full life for 33 years after that. In the meantime, our children, Dinesh cleared engineering and started working and Satya became a doctor and joined Sankara Netralaya. Both of them got married. But God took away my mother in law after 3 months of Satya's marriage. Then came the day when Chatu had a massive heart attack 4 days after his mother passed away. He was admitted to National Heart Institute, Kailash Colony.

Being the only son, apple of the eye, he could not accept Bhabhi, my mother-in-law not being there anymore. All his four sisters the eldest Mohini Didi, Padma Didi, Papu Didi and Usha loved their brother a lot. Though he never expressed the emotion, he felt for his sisters, he loved them a lot too.

After he was hospitalised several times for high pulse rates, the doctors decided to implant ICD. In his lifetime 3 ICD's were implanted with a gap of 9 years each in between. The life of the battery in the ICD lasted for 8-9 years depending on the number of episodes of high pulse rates. This pacemaker did the work of suppressing the high pulse and thus it was set at 70. He was the first role model to have ICD in their hospital at Dr. Padmavati's National Heart Institute.

He went under the knife several times. He had colon cancer and was operated, 10" of his large intestine was removed. We all stood by him and he became normal within months. When he was in operation theatre & was being operated, the effect of anaesthesia was over but he bore the pain of the operation without any complaint.

He was so nice, he encouraged me to go abroad to Dubai once, and thrice to USA to meet my sisters, even though he could not travel due to health reasons.

Both my sons are the true copy of their father. Honest, quiet and helpful. They do not have any of my qualities in them. They are now my backbone. God bless them.

Sometimes I feel God chose me to be Chatu's partner, thinking this girl will look after him well. And I was never tired of looking after him and his diet.

Throughout the journey together we came across lots of nice people whom we had never met before, but because of his nature they went out of their way to help him. One such incident I remember vividly was when we were travelling to USA for the first time for his bypass surgery. We had a halt of 8 hrs at Heathrow Airport. I was asked to give him food every 2 hrs as he was very weak. I had no Sterling pounds to buy him food at Heathrow Airport. So, God sent me a good samaritan in the form of the attendant of his wheelchair. I happened to tell him about this condition, so he took us to the business lounge at the Airport and asked us to partake as much as we liked. I still remember him a lot. He was a very tall, dark & handsome African person.

Then we landed in Chicago and admitted him in the hospital. 10 doctors sat to decide for the surgery after the angiography. 9 said no surgery is needed, only one said yes. But the most wonderful thing was they refused to take the fees. They said there was something God like in him. He was just asked to take half aspirin daily.

I always called him second Gandhi of India. He had that superpower of bearing the pain & facing the turbulences that came in his life. He always had that charming personality of attracting people towards him. I never heard him talking bitterly about anyone. Wherever he went people were in all praises for him. His office staff in CPWD, NBCC and on construction in Yemen all praised him a lot. He would allow ladies to leave for home early if they had problems at home.

Today is 20th June, 2021 – Father's Day. My grand daughter baked cupcakes in her Dadu's name and we all had them together celebrating Father's Day. His birthday falls on July 30. He will be 87 years this year.

Chatu and myself with Dinesh, Ruby and Ishita

So, he has stepped down and left the seat near me vacant and perhaps so will I leave the seat of mine and join him. He will be fondly remembered by one and all the passengers we met on the train of life. We all miss him a lot.

According to Bhagwat Gita, our entire life is Yajna means offering self-sacrifice. You pour out everything to worship the Almighty. He in turn helps you in getting rid of the bondage of rebirth and many lives of suffering.

Living in a noble way in the spirit of "Work is worship" which I believe we are here to do and perform well. It is about conducting oneself in such a way that it becomes an example to others, without desire for any reward, exerting themselves for the sake of duty. He performed his duty very well.

57 years was a long period of life together with him. Life is never fully under control. It keeps throwing surprises. Why not accept the cycle of pleasant & unpleasant events and move on. Life henceforth will not be a bed of roses, but have to go along with my children

God called your name so gently that only you could hear. No one heard the footsteps of the angel coming near. You closed your eyes and went to sleep forever. You quietly left us all. Hare Ram.

God saw you getting tired when a cure was not in sight. He wrapped his arms around you and whispered "Come unto me". You didn't deserve what you went through and so He gave you rest. God's garden must be beautiful. He only takes the best. So, when I saw you sleeping so peacefully and free from pain at last, I could not wish you to come back to suffer all that again.

God sent me to him to look after him with dedication till the end. I tried to fulfil his wishes all our life. People thought I was pampering him but I knew he needed me the most and I was the one chosen to look after him. We were together for 57 years. How time flies. Then came the day when we had to part and he left me to go and serve God in heaven. The world is this stage where we come, perform and leave. As a husband, father and son he was a wonderful man. May God bless him wherever he is.

The mystery to everyone is we do not know at which station we ourselves will step down this train of life. We must live the best way, love, forgive and offer the best who we are. Lastly, I thank you for being one of the passengers on my train. Sai Ram.

Contents